HOW TO MANAGE KINDLE CONTENT AND DEVICES

A Concised Beginner to Pro Handbook on How to Manage Your Contents and Device in 5 minutes (Picture Guide)

ADAMS G. CROSS

COPYRIGHT

TABLE OF CONTENT

CHAPTER ONE

INTRODUCTION

Many Amazon Kindle owners explore the kindle app on their laptops, smartphone, or tablet and they do not only set up a lot of devices with the Kindle app, but also snagged a lot of ebooks and different content material from Amazon.

Now a big question is asked, *how do you manage that and all your Kindle devices?*

Amazon is a committed webpage the place you can view and manage your Kindle. At this page, you can cast off Kindle devices you no longer use. Additionally, you can switch Kindle ebooks from one device to another and delete several eBooks and content that are of no use anymore

The Kindle app is a versatile application, this is because it can be accessed on Kindle devices, Computers, macOS, Android and iOS.

What this means is that you can read and download lots of Kindle ebooks on simply about any platform. As soon as you download a Kindle ebook, Amazon even asks which machine you want it to land on, showing you a list of all the devices you no longer use or you may have ebooks that you no longer read or have need for. The steps to disposing off and managing your kindle content and devices quite simple.

CHAPTER TWO

HOW TO MANAGE CONTENT AND DEVICES PAINLESSLY

In a bid to make managing kindle content and device easy, several screenshots have been taken with instructions to guide you through.

The first thing to do is to get into you account on the Amazon website.

To do this, click on "Your Account"

Click on "Manage Your Content and Devices"

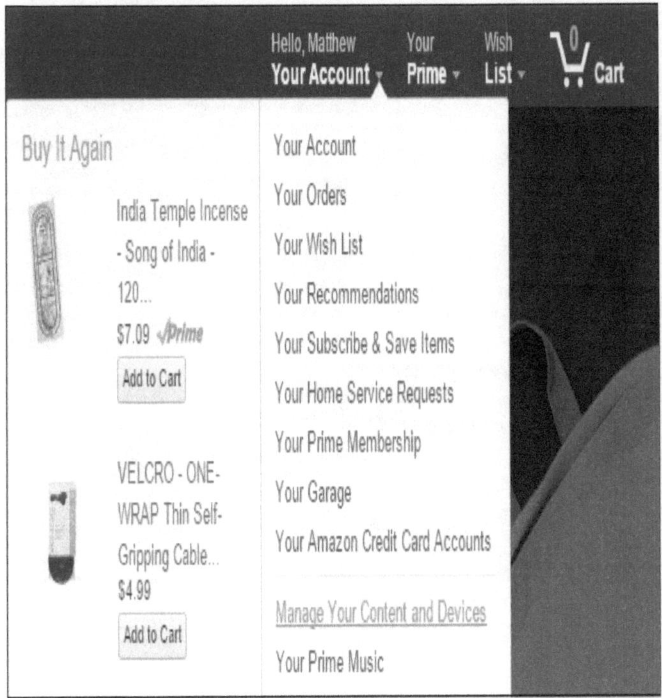

The next thing to do is to sign in to your account.

amazon
Your Account | Help
Sign In
What is your e-mail or mobile number?
E-mail or mobile number:
Do you have an Amazon.com password?
No, I am a new customer.
Yes, I have a password:
Forgot your password?
Sign in using our secure server

The screenshot below is the next section that appears after signing in, showing you your eBooks.

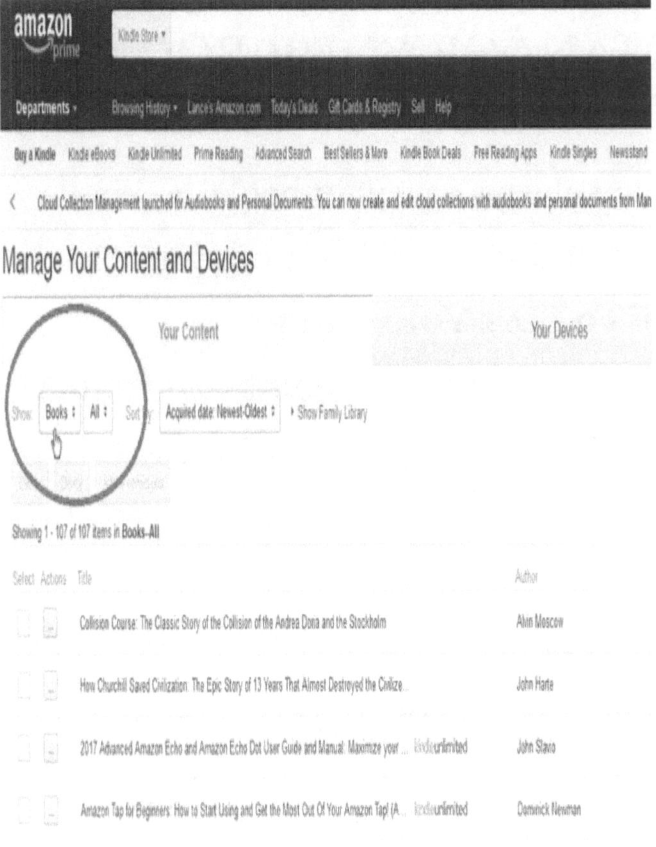

CHAPTER THREE

HOW TO SORT AND MANAGE YOUR BOOKS WITHOUT STRESS

You can always sort your books on kindle for easy location and identification.

How To Sort Your Books

You can choose to sort your books from A-Z, Z-A, Oldest to Newest, or Newest to Oldest.

Simply click on the drox box to display the various options and select the one that suits you.

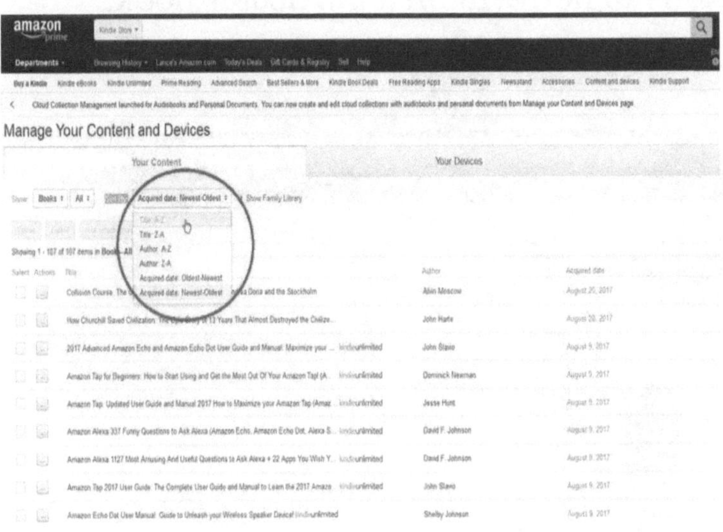

How To Manage Your Books

Click on the "Action" button to display options to perform on a particular book.

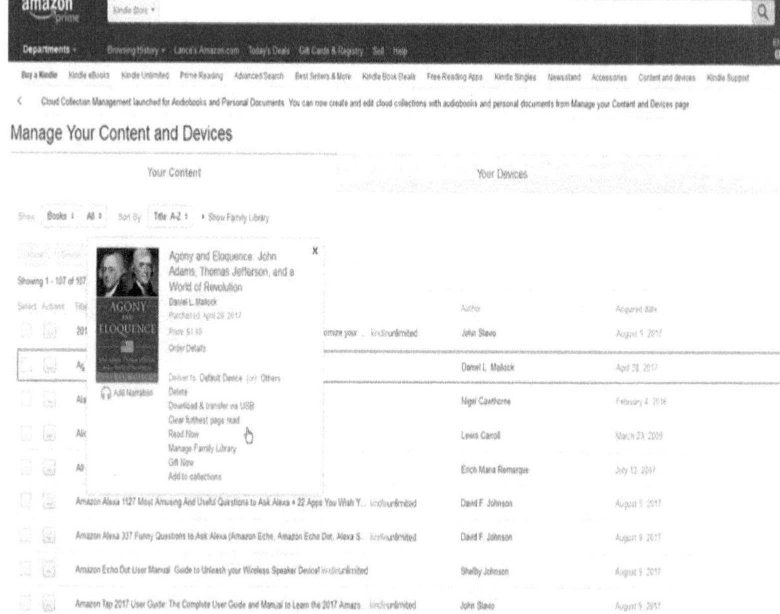

CHAPTER FOUR

HOW TO SPEEDILY DILIVER A CONTENT TO A DEVICE

You can always send books or other content to other devices on the Amazon account.

To deliver a book to another device, select the book and click on "Deliver"

Next, confirm the delivery action

CHAPTER FIVE

HOW TO DELETE BOOKS IN SECONDS

Deleting unwanted books off your Amazon account permanently is one easy thing to do.

Simply select the book or books you no longer want and hit "Delete" button at the top.

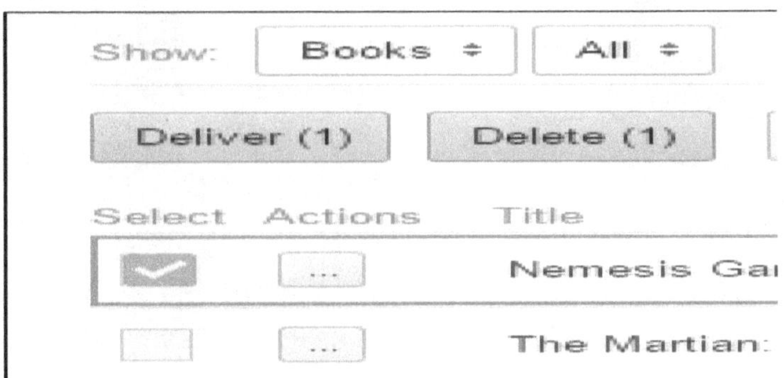

Next, confirm your delete action by clicking on "Yes, delete permanently"

Remember if you delete this book, it will go out from all your devices.

CHAPTER SIX

EASIEST WAY TO DOWNLOADING AND RETURNING BOOKS

It is very easy to download an return book you don't need.

Click on the Download button to get the
book to your app and confirm the
download action after select the preferred
device.

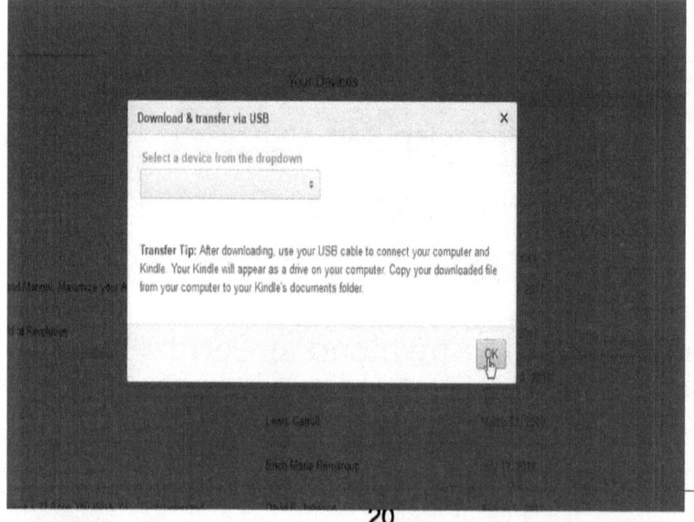

To return the bvook, just click on the return button and confirm the action.

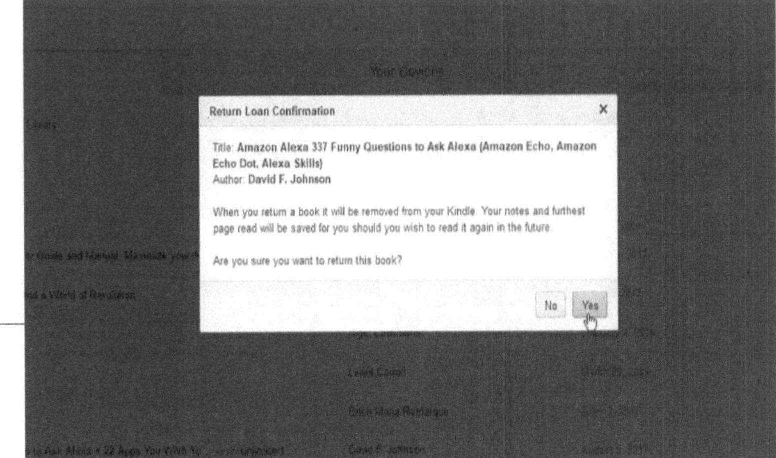

CHAPTER SEVEN

READING BOOKS ON YOUR DEVICE

You can decide to read books on your computer by clicking on the "Read Now" button.

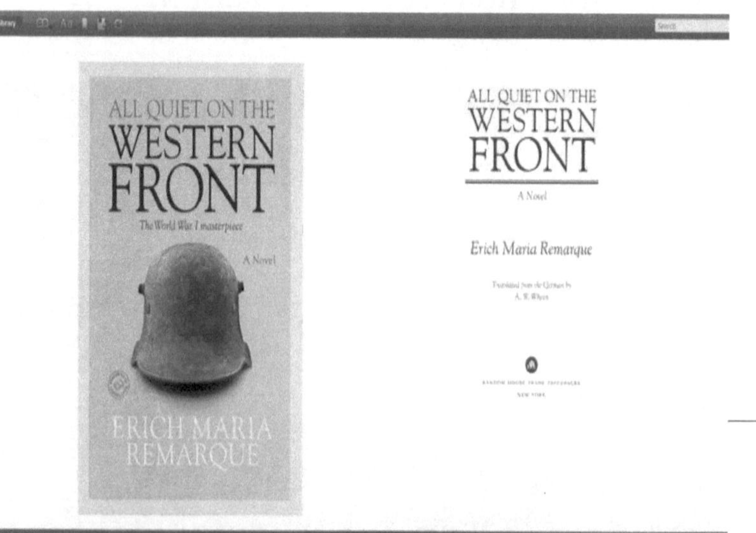

CHAPTER EIGHT

HOW TO EASILY MANAGE FAMILY LIBRARY

When you have set up the a family library on your Amazon kindle tablet, you can always click on the "Manage Family Library" to add or send more books to the household library.

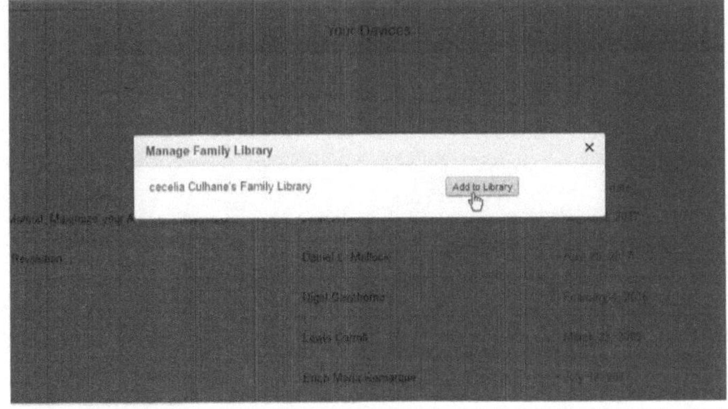

CHAPTER NINE

GIFTING SOMEONE A BOOK WITHOUT STRESS

You can also send loved ones a book as a gift.
Just click on "Give Now"

Next, fill out the necessary information and confirm it.

amazon.com

Complete your gift purchase

Review the information below, then click "Place your order."   Place your order

● Email the gift directly to my recipient

Email address: ___________________ (joe@example.com)

Delivery date: Now
Your gift will be sent between 12:00am and 3:00am Pacific Time on the date selected.
(mm/dd/yyyy)

○ Email the gift to me
You can forward the gift email or print and personally deliver it to the recipient.

Order Summary
Subtotal*: $0.99

1-Click Payment method:

Billing address:
Lance Whitney

Change

Personalize your message (optional)

Recipient name: ___________________

Your name: Lance Whitney

Message: ___________________

300 characters remaining. Plain text only.

Preview Email

Alan Turing: The Enigma Man (Kindle Edition)
by Nigel Cawthorne

The recipient can exchange your gift for an equivalent value Amazon.com gift card. Title availability may vary by country. If this title isn't available for your gift recipient, we will exchange your gift for an equivalent value Amazon.com gift card. If you have selected "Now" as the delivery date, your payment will be processed and your gift will be delivered immediately upon clicking "Place Your Order."

*Eligible gift card or promotional credit will automatically be applied to your order. The sales tax ultimately charged will be calculated when your charge is authorized and will reflect any applicable state and local taxes.

Place your order

CHAPTER TEN

PLACING YOUR BOOKS IN DIFFERENT CATEGORIES FOR QUICK LOCATION

When all your downloaded or purchased books are in a single folder, it makes it look untidy. To organise it for an easy access and identification, simply create new collections and move your books accordingly.

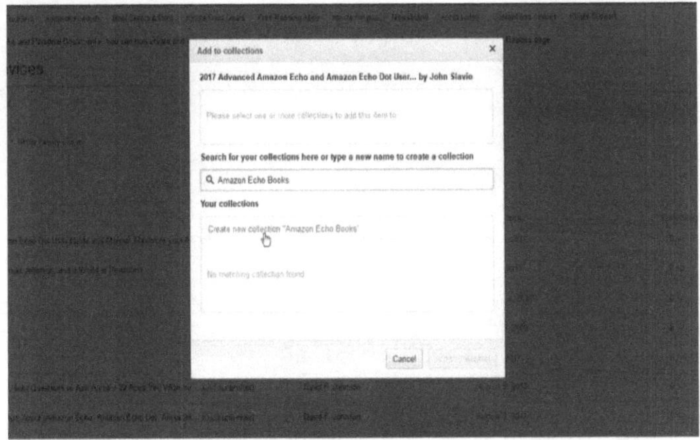

CHAPTER ELEVEN

SELECTING MANY BOOKS FOR AN ACTION

If you need to delete, deliver or add several books to a collection or category, you can select many books and hit on the required action button to proceed.

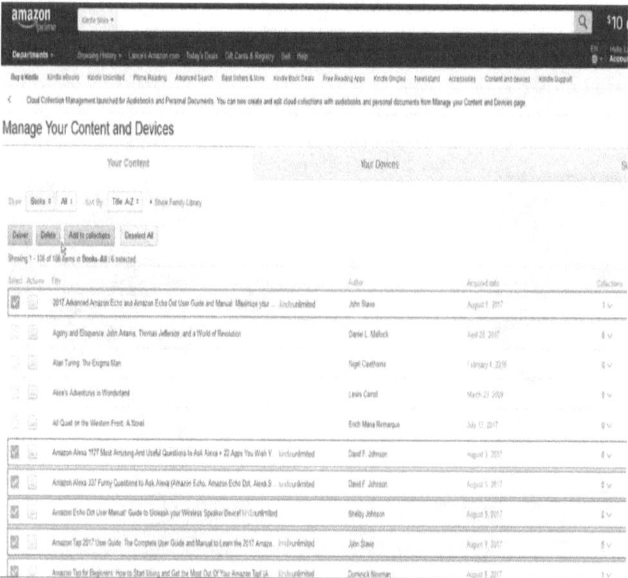

CHAPTER TWELVE

VIEWING AND EDITING OTHER MEDIA CONTENT WITHOUT STRESS

Apart from reading or viewing books on kindle, you can also view other media contents.
Just click on the menu close to "Show", it will show you different media content, you can choose either video, audio, magazines or any other items you have downloaded or purchased.

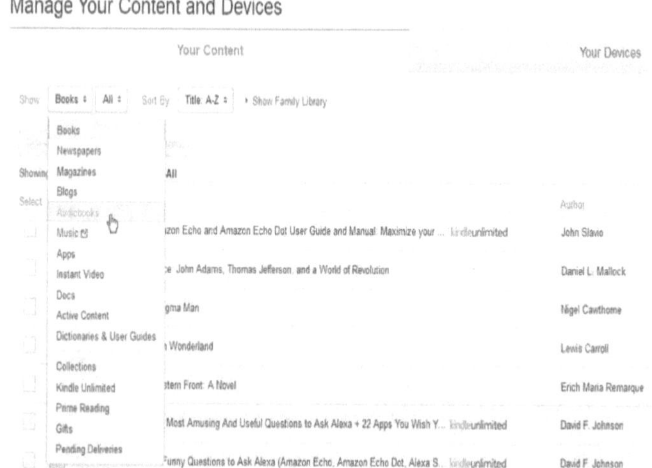

Editing other media is simply doing similar actions, either delete, deliver, add to collections or any other.

Manage Your Content and Devices

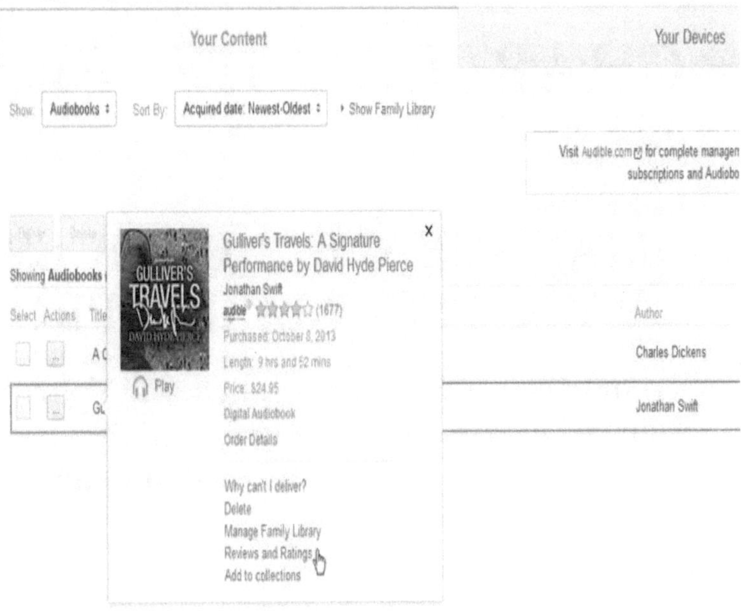

CHAPTER THIRTEEN

MANAGE YOUR DEVICES PAINLESSLY LIKE A PRO

To manage your devices, click on "Your Device" at the top and a list of all device registered to your account will appear.

Deleting A Device

To delete a device that is registered to your account, simply click on "Deregister"

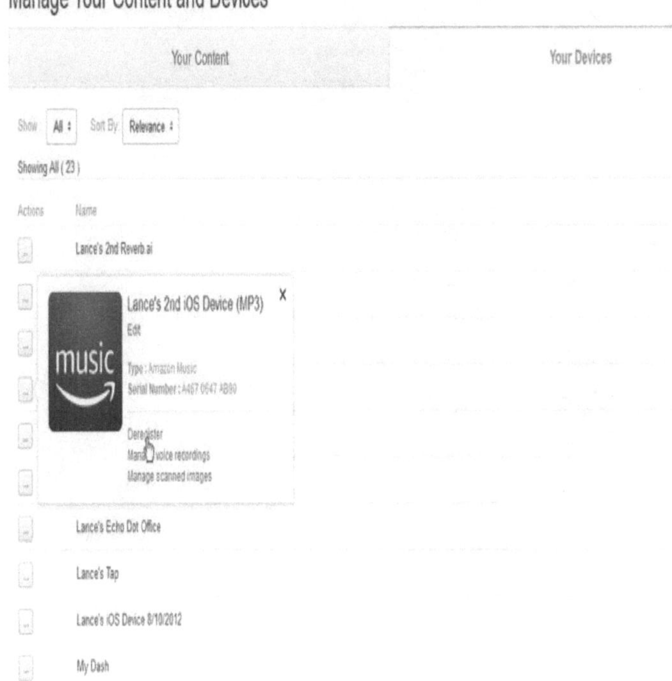

Setting A Default Device
Just tap "set as default device" to carryout this action.

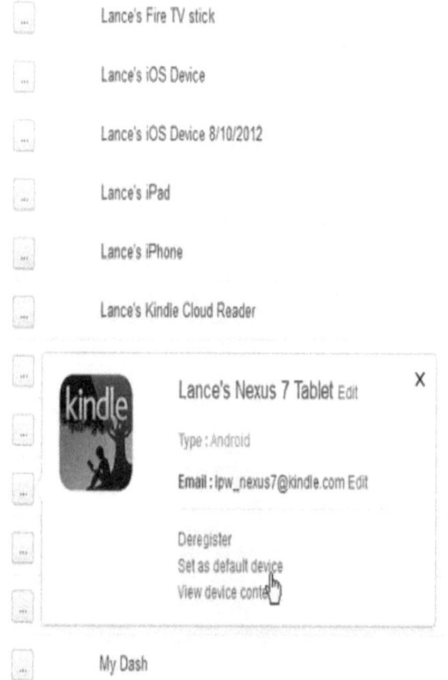

Setting Up Your Account

Lastly, you can do several account setting like payment method, ghousehold or family library, language and other by clicking on "Settings"

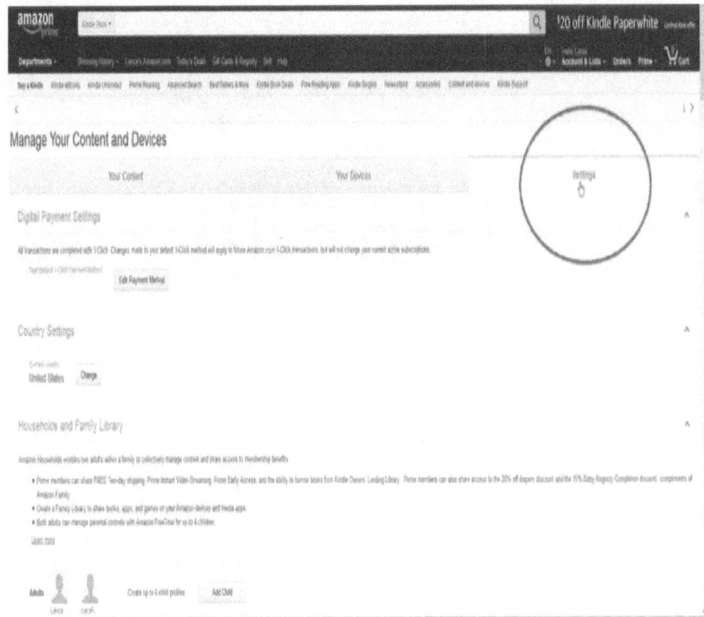

THE END